From Trash to Treasures

Plastic

Daniel Nunn

Heinemann Library
Chicago, Illinois

www.heinemannraintree.com
Visit our website to find out
more information about
Heinemann-Raintree books.

To order:

☎ Phone 888-454-2279

💻 Visit www.heinemannraintree.com
to browse our catalog and order online.

Edited by Rebecca Rissman, Daniel Nunn, and
Sian Smith
Designed by Joanna Hinton-Malivoire
Picture research by Tracy Cummins
Originated by Capstone Global Library Ltd
Printed in China

15 14 13 12
10 9 8 7 6 5 4 3 2

**Library of Congress Cataloging-in-Publication
Data**
Nunn, Daniel.
  Plastic / Daniel Nunn.
    p. cm.—(From trash to treasures)
  Includes bibliographical references and index.
  ISBN 978-1-4329-5148-1 (hc)—ISBN 978-1-4329-
5157-3 (pb) 1. Plastics craft—Juvenile literature. 2.
Plastics—Recycling—Juvenile literature. 3. Recycled
products—Juvenile literature. I. Title.
  TT297.N86 2012
  745.57'2—dc22   2010049815

Acknowledgments
We would like to thank the following for permission
to reproduce photographs: Alamy p. 22a (©
PhotoStock-Israel); Corbis pp. 9, 23b (© BRIAN
SNYDER/Reuters); Heinemann Raintree pp. 4, 22c,
23e (David Rigg), 5, 6, 8, 10, 11, 12, 13, 14, 15, 16, 17,
18, 19, 20, 21, 23f (Karon Dubke); istockphoto pp. 7
(© westphalia), 22b (© subjug); Shutterstock pp.
23a (© GJS), 23c (© homydesign), 23d (© Alaettin
YILDIRIM), 23f (© Losevsky Pavel).

Cover photograph of artwork made from plastic
bags reproduced with permission of Photolibrary
(Heiner Heine). Cover inset image of plastic bags
reproduced with permission of istockphoto
(© NoDerog). Back cover photographs of a piggy
bank and a parachute reproduced with permission
of Heinemann Raintree (Karon Dubke).

Every effort has been made to contact copyright
holders of material reproduced in this book. Any
omissions will be rectified in subsequent printings if
notice is given to the publisher.

Disclaimer
All the Internet addresses (URLs) given in this book
were valid at the time of going to press. However,
due to the dynamic nature of the Internet, some
addresses may have changed, or sites may have
changed or ceased to exist since publication. While
the author and publisher regret any inconvenience
this may cause readers, no responsibility for any
such changes can be accepted by either the
author or the publisher.

Contents

Some words are shown in bold, **like this**. You can find them in the glossary on page 23.

What Is Plastic?

Plastic is a human-made **material**. It can be made into lots of different shapes.

Plastic is often used in **packaging**.

When you buy food or drinks from a store, they often come in plastic **containers**.

Water bottles, yogurt cups, and margarine tubs are all made of plastic.

What Happens When You Throw Plastic Away?

Plastic is very useful.

But when you have finished with it, do you throw it away?

If you throw plastic away, it will end up at a garbage dump.

It will be buried in the ground and may stay there for a very long time.

What Is Recycling?

It is much better to **recycle** plastic than to throw it away.

Separate plastic things from your other trash and put them in a recycling bin.

The plastic things will be collected and taken to a **factory**.

Then the plastic will be made into something new.

How Can I Reuse Old Plastic?

You can also use old plastic to make your own new things.

When you have finished with a plastic bag, bottle, or **container**, put it away somewhere instead of throwing it away.

Soon you will have lots of plastic waiting to be reused.

You are ready to turn your trash into treasures!

What Can I Make with Plastic Bottles?

Plastic bottles are used to hold **liquids** like milk or soda.

But you can use them to make fun piggy banks.

You can also use them to make some spooky lanterns.

It is easy to light them up using battery-powered candles.

What Can I Make with Plastic Containers?

Old yogurt cups make perfect plant pots for herbs.

Plant a different herb in each pot, and remember to make them look nice!

You can use an ice cream tub to make a beautiful gift basket for someone special.

What will you put in yours?

What Can I Make with Plastic Bags?

Plastic bags can be used to make all sorts of things.

They can be knitted into bags and purses.

You can also use them to make
parachutes for your toys.

But remember, you must NEVER put
plastic bags over your head.

Make Your Own Yogurt-Cup Animals

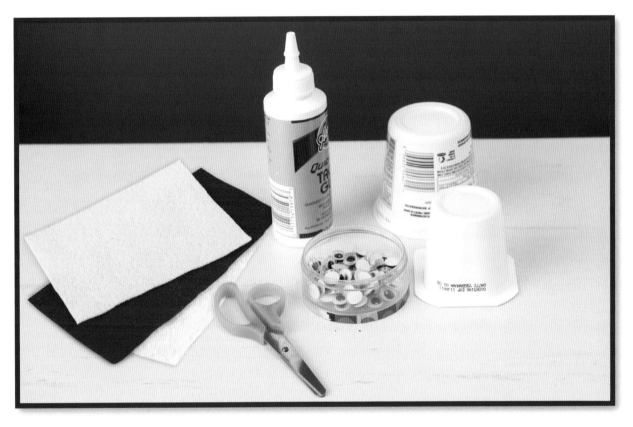

You can use old yogurt cups to make your own fun animals.

You will need some empty yogurt cups, pieces of **felt** in different colors, googly eyes, scissors, and some glue.

First, cut a large piece of felt to glue around the yogurt cup.

You could use white for a rabbit, red for a ladybug, or black pieces for a cow.

Next, cut some ears, a nose, and a mouth and glue them onto your animal.

Finally, remember to glue on your animal's eyes!

You have now finished making your first yogurt-cup animal.

Now it's time to make it some friends!

Recycling Quiz

One of these things is made from **recycled** plastic. Can you guess which one? (The answer is on page 24.)

Glossary

 **container** object used to put things in

 **factory** building where something is made

 **felt** type of cloth, often used in crafts

 **liquid** substance that can flow, like water or oil

 **material** what something is made of

 **packaging** box or wrapping that something comes in

 **recycle** break down a material and use it again to make something new

Find Out More

Ask an adult to help you make fun things with plastic using the Websites below.

Piggy bank: **www.freekidscrafts.com/index. php?option=com_events&task=view_detail&agid=599**

Toy parachutes: **http://familyfun.go.com/playtime/ plastic-bag-paratrooper-708602/**

You can find other ideas at: **http://enchantedlearning. com/crafts/straws/**

Answer to question on page 22
The clothes are made from recycled plastic.

Index